Laying the Groundwork for Revival among the Maasai in Africa

"The land of Zebulun and the land of Naphtali, by the way of the sea, beyond Jordan, Galilee of the Gentiles: the people who sat in great darkness have seen a great light, and upon those who sat in the region and shadow of death light has dawned."
Matthew 4:15,16

Dalen Garris
RevivalFire Ministries

This is a work of history. Historical individuals and places and events are mentioned.

Copyright © 2021 by Dalen Garris

Cover design by Renee Garris

Published by Revivalfire Ministries

ISBN 13: 978-1-7377944-3-1

*All rights reserved.
No part of this book may be used or reproduced in any manner whatsoever, without written permission, except in the case of brief quotations embodied in critical articles and reviews, as provided by U.S. Copyright Law.*

*For information, address
dale@revivalfire.org*

First paperback printing November 2021

Printed in the United States of America

Table of Contents_Toc85039376

Introduction	1
1 - The Maasai	3
2 - Hungry Hearts	6
3 - Light in a Dark Room	9
4 - The Proclaimers	12
5 - Hakuna Matata	15
6 – Remote Areas	18
7 – Services by Kerosene Lantern	20
8 - A Great Light	22
9 - Services in the Bush	25
10 - Arusha	28
11- African Nights	30
12 – The Barbaig	33
13 – Fleas in the Night	37
14 – A Hard Gospel	39
15 - Explosion	42
16 - Miracles and the Message	45
17 - A Great Light	49

Introduction

*"I'm sitting here in a railway station,
Got a ticket for my destination ..."*
Paul Simon

This should all be routine by now. Six trips to Africa should make me, if not a veteran, at least used to this, but there has been an anticipation to this trip for the last month that is not showing any signs of dissipating. Is there something different about this trip? What is ahead of me during the next month in the back bush country of the Maasai tribe?

Sitting here at the airport, waiting for my flight, business people and tourists are all around me, scurrying to one place or another in an unending rush to go somewhere. I sometimes sit and wonder what their private lives are like – are they stressed, are they happy, are they just average folks just like me, or are they on a special mission in their lives?

The mission that is before me seems to loom much bigger than myself. I am not going on some cute little mission trip. This is not to "minister" to some villagers out in the bush and come back satisfied that I helped the indigent in some way – this is a mission to wage war against an enemy who has had a strong grip in these areas for thousands of years and is not ready to give it up. I am going there to lay the groundwork for revival.

Judging by the fire we have gone through for the last month, since the very day I purchased the ticket, this will be a humdinger of a fight. We have plowed through one difficulty after the other, day after day, knowing that each battle has its own victory, but it also has its own price to pay.

Hopefully, the girls in the office will be able to get a break from the constant drizzle of problems that fall on each day. They are actually glad to see me go, just so they can get some relief.

As I prepare to board the plane, I feel exhausted already, but glad that the preliminaries, at least, are over.

1 - *The Maasai*

The one thing I may remember the most about this trip to Africa is the red dust. It feels like I am on Mars – everywhere you look, you are surrounded by the same red dirt that you see in NASA pictures. And it's just about as dry.

We are in Namanga, a small town on the border of Kenya and Tanzania, remote from the bustle of Nairobi and deep in Maasai land. The streets look like something out of a Western movie, complete with the wooden storefronts, dusty red dirt streets, and goats and sheep wandering around the main street. You almost expect to see cowboys ride into town at any moment.

Instead of seeing Indians, the entire scene is garnished with the bright colors of native Maasai in their traditional garb – garments of bright reds and brilliant colors that they wrap themselves in like a bedsheet and punctuated with staccato bursts of color throughout the beaded collars, wrist and ankle bands, and loops of ear jewelry that puncture the holes cut into their ears. It is like nothing you've ever seen.

The Maasai are a proud and strong people, rich in culture and tradition, and uninfluenced by the modern society that grows around them. Most notable for their traditional dress and beaded jewelry, they stand out in any crowd, even in the midst of Africa. But it is the strength of their character and the depth of their closed tribal culture that impresses me more than their startling appearance.

They do not possess fear like most people, and stories abound of their confrontation with lions and other beasts of prey. Lions are afraid of Maasai if that tells you anything.

Money holds no meaning for them, only their cattle, and they feel that all cattle belong to them, especially if they are owned by someone that is not Maasai. The things that do matter to them have to do with their tribal and family bonds, and that is what maintains their separation from the rest of the world. They are Maasai. They are not like everyone else.

The traditions of the elders maintain such a strong grip that Christianity has had a difficult time making inroads here. They have their own pagan religion that they strongly cling to, and, although I haven't learned much about it yet, I suspect that it is deeply strange, dark, and unique.

Nevertheless, once a Maasai gets saved, the transformation and the spiritual burst of freedom transforms them, and they will cling as strongly to their newly found faith as they did their old pagan traditions. It is quite a transformation to see.

And see it, I shall. This month will be filled with services two and three times a day in churches and villages out in the bush where the Gospel is beginning to take root. I am excited and fully expect to see not only the miracles that usually attend such meetings, but a great outpouring of the Spirit of God that will energize this entire area. This is exactly the kind of situation where God loves to show up in great power and glory.

Who knows what God will do here? I know that revival is coming to this region of Africa, so maybe this will be the match that He strikes to start the fire. Wouldn't it be just like God to do something totally unexpected in such an unusual and remote place with a people that no one would have guessed would be the ones He would use to light the torch?

Yeah, that would be just like God to astound everyone and choose the foolish things of the world to confound the wise.

2 - *Hungry Hearts*

I can hardly believe that I am here in Africa. Sometimes it almost feels surreal. I am out in the bush country of Africa, riding in the back of a mini pickup truck, driving down a bouncy dirt track, dodging huge thorn bushes, in and out of deep washed-out gullies.

In a way, this almost looks like the desert country of Arizona or West Texas. It hasn't rained in this place since I was here last Spring, so it has that same arid feel to it. The dust wafts through the air and you can feel the grit dig into your skin.

Somehow, we reach a small Anglican church out in the middle of nowhere. How people don't get lost out here is beyond me. Looking out into the landscape of unbroken bush, I wonder how anyone will know how to come here. And where are they coming from? There are no houses out here!

But they do come. Services begin to warm up while the women cook dinner and tea over a campfire, which is traditionally served after services. It's almost like a family affair where everyone gathers together to have church, dinner, and fellowship.

The second service is held up on a hill closer to the suburbs of town. We are still in an area where there is no water or power, where the homes are small 15 ft. square mud buildings with corrugated tin roofs. They're not much to look at, but this is home for most of Africa's population.

The church is the same kind of building – a little square building made of wooden poles that are packed with a hard dried mud. Windows are a square hole in the walls, and the door is made with rough-hewn boards nailed together.

But inside, there is a cheery atmosphere. The place is packed wall-to-wall with people from all over who have come to hear the Mzungu (white man) bring forth the Word of God. It would be an understatement to say that I am an oddity.

It was the third service today that was the one that was the most powerful.

Believe it or not, there were only 3 people that showed up. I am used to this by now, so we just dove into the services, singing and dancing to clapping and the beating of a drum. The rest of the people would come later, moving in African time (Hakuna Matata). Nevertheless, even with all the late additions, there are only a handful of people by the time we begin to close services.

The songs have been sung, the message has been given, and the testimonies delivered … but we can't close. The Spirit of God will not let us. The Holy Spirit starts pouring – I mean POURING – down on us, and instead of a closing prayer and benediction, we keep praying and praying and praying. Before you know it, some people are up on their feet, marching back and forth, praying at the top of their lungs, while others are on their faces before God down on the floor.

And we just keep praying…

I don't' know how long this went on – time is difficult to gauge when the power of the Holy Ghost is flowing – but when it was finally over, everyone was changed.

I've been in a lot of services like this, and there is never any warning. It just happens. The preparation for such a visitation from God has little to do with the service, and everything to do with people's hearts.

These are hungry hearts, and God has fed them.

3 - Light in a Dark Room

My day has started with another excursion into the bush. Namanga is a small city in the middle of a semi-arid area. Within a mile of town, the landscape turns dusty, dry, and barren except for the thorny acacia trees that cover the area just like mesquite trees in Texas.

There are few roads, if any, in this place. The dirt tracks are more for cattle and goats than wheeled vehicles. I know people live out here somewhere, but there are few signs other than an occasional group of cattle with a lone Maasai herdsman standing silently on the side watching us pass.

It should be no surprise that the population is so sparse. The drought that has taken over this land has devastated the land. No rain for over six or seven months has turned the soil to dust, and the grass to brittle straw. The cattle, which are the mainstay of life for these Maasai, are dying from lack of water. Even the sturdy acacia trees have shed their leaves, adding to the barrenness.

We arrive suddenly at the church. Again, we are out in the middle of nowhere, and I have no idea how a church got built way out here. Where do all the people live? How do they know to come here for church, never mind how they even know how to get here without getting lost?

To answer my questions, the pastor takes me down the road to a traditional Maasai home. After walking about a half-mile, we come to a wall of thorny branches piled 4 ft. high in a huge circle surrounding a handful of mud huts. I am told that even lions will not get through these barriers. The thorns are three inches long, and trust me, they are sharp!

I am invited to crawl into a hut. The place is only 4 feet high, and the door is about 18 inches wide. As I squeeze in, I see that it is like a compressed hallway, 4 ft. high and 2 ft. wide, that twists and turns into the room. It is a little claustrophobic for me.

The room is shadowy dark with a small campfire burning in the center. I stumble into the gloom and find a ledge to sit on. A little toothless woman sits in the middle of a 5 ft. diameter room, tending the fire. She smiles. The ledge I am sitting on is her bed. The man's ledge is on the other side.

I feel like I am in the home of a Hobbit – but one that lurks in darkness. It is so dark that it takes time for my eyes to adjust. The "windows" are two 3" holes – that's it, nothing else. There is no room to stretch or even sit up straight. And I'm not sure what I would bump into if I did, or if the whole place would fall in. Real cozy.

Back to the church, we find people have been filtering in from the bush and a small crowd is waiting for me. I have brought with me an audio player with talking Bible in the Maasai language. As the pastor shows them how it works, their excitement switches on like a light. Here is the Word of God spoken in their own language that they can listen to. Few have a formal education and have learned to read, so this is an incredible blessing.

This is where it strikes me how important this is. Imagine believing that Jesus Christ is Lord. You have been saved and have felt the Spirit of God change your life. You know that it is the truth and that the Bible is God's Word and is vital for your spiritual life – but you cannot read so you are cut off from the very thing that can give you life. It's as if you are groping about in a dark room looking for the door that opens to the outside.

And then some white guy from Texas comes and gives you the key that opens the door to Truth, a lamp that sheds the darkness, and the Bread of Life to feed your starving soul. All of a sudden, the brightness of God's Word shines in your life.

Wow. It doesn't get much better than this. This has to be the best job in the entire world.

4 - The Proclaimers

Mornings here in Kenya have a startling clarity to them. The sunshine directly overhead cuts through the air with a sharp focus. Even the air smells crisp.

Every morning, I walk across the street to an outside café for my instant Nescafe and mandazi, a traditional baked roll. This morning, however, the café is closed for the Islamic holiday of Ramadan, so I've had to make my way down the street to another café to take my coffee there and soak up the morning's fresh breeze.

Yesterday's services are still fresh in my mind – one in a little mud church out in the bush, and another in town. Each service so far has had its own individual personality and its own message.

The afternoon service started normally. You could see the Maasai filtering in through the bush, dressed in their brightly colored robes. I wonder what they are expecting. What will the Mzungu have for them? Am I just a curiosity, or are their hearts hoping for something that will break through the average monotony of life?

One thing that does excite them is the Proclaimer audio player that I have brought. You should see Rev. Sampao, my Maasai host, as he excitedly explains how this can play the Bible in the Maasai language! And it is not dependent on electricity because it has a solar panel and an auxiliary hand crank! They laugh and applaud as he dances around the room, turning the hand crank to show them.

This is a very big deal. Most of these people cannot read, so this is a miraculous opening of God's Word to them. Their only exposure to the Bible up until now has been confined to scattered glimpses when someone else shares their Bible with them.

Americans do not understand the depth of this situation. It is difficult for us to comprehend the challenges that face these Christians who are immersed in a land of spiritual darkness and witchcraft, surrounded by Islam, and yet forced to stand strong in their faith without a Bible to read. And here comes this American who has not only brought Bibles but has given them the spoken Word so they can listen to God's Word in their own language. It's like ripping open the curtains in a dark room to open up a big bay window and have the bright sunlight of the noon day come blasting in, flooding your soul with God's glory.

I guarantee you that, if you were to come here with me just one time, you would never be the same ever again. The feeling is overwhelming. It swells your heart so much that you can hardly speak.

One Pastor has told me that, of the 45 people in his church, he is the only one who has a Bible, and 30 of those 45 can't read. So how does he feed them the Word of God? Every Sunday, he passes the Bible around so that each member can read a verse, and then pass it on to the next person. That way, he tells me, they can all get a chance to "see how good it feels to read the Word of God".

Can you grasp this? To read a verse just so you can have a chance to see how good the Word of God feels?

May God have mercy on us who take our freedom and prosperity for granted.

And may God grant us the grace to not pass over the desperation of these hungry souls, and to keep us from the complacency of ignoring a call to provide Bibles.

"Whoso stoppeth his ears at the cry of the poor, he also shall cry himself, but shall not be heard."
Proverbs 21:13

5 - *Hakuna Matata*

I have been to several churches this week, and it is pretty much the same routine – sing songs, hand out Bibles, preach, and, of course, take pictures. The songs are always the same – I'm not always sure what they are saying, but they sing it over and over.

"Ni wewe, Ni wewe Bwana" (it is you; it is you Lord)

"Halleluyah, tu mwambia Bwana, A'sante" (Halleluyah, Let us tell Him, Lord, Thank you)

While the repertoire may be a bit shallow, the passion and feeling with which they sing are not. In a short time, the passion begins to rise, and soon the whole place is throbbing with the rhythm of these Gospel songs that are peculiar to Africa. The singing lasts an hour before we move on to giving them the Bibles and the Proclaimer, a talking Bible player with the New Testament in their language.

I know I have already told you about the deep effect that these Bibles have, but it is worth mentioning again that this is one of the biggest things to happen in their lives (next to getting saved, of course). A pastor stopped us last night to tell us how one of his members broke out in tears when he gave her one of our Bibles. It is a life-changing moment – for both them and me.

African people live close to the soil, and as a result, are an earthy people. It tends to simplify everything – from their economics to their perspectives about life in general. Their way of life is not only simpler, but their entire pace is also slower and easier. Hakuna Matata ("no worries"); "There's no hurry in Africa".

It takes some time to get used to their way of doing things, but I am slowly coming around. After a while, you begin to wonder why we Americans are rushing around about at such a furious pace. Maybe they are on to something here.

But then again, it also limits their perspectives in space and in time. They look inside their immediate horizon to see only the things that concern them right now. Anything beyond their horizon will be dealt with when it happens. Until then, well, hakuna matata.

It is the same with time. The present is a reality; the future has not yet fallen within that circumscribed arena. They will worry about the future when it happens.

Maybe this is not such a bad way to live. No worries; no problems. Life will always work itself out. And it usually does. But I am not here to relax. I am here to lay the groundwork for a revival amongst the Maasai, and that lack of urgency in their lives is one of the greatest challenges that faces me. Revival never comes to people who are satisfied. It only comes to those who are desperate for a move from God and are willing to pay the price to get one.

The hearts of these people are rich and fertile with a deep, sincere need for God, and with that, God can work miracles.

And I am seeing it begin in one church at a time.

6 – Remote Areas

I have no idea where I am. I don't even know which country I am in right now. I do know that we are about forty to fifty miles from the nearest paved road, following dirt roads and tracks to churches way out in the bush.

The last few days have been a monotonous landscape of hard-packed red dirt, acacia thorn trees, and dry dust. You see birds, but few other animals other than an occasional gazelle or ground squirrel (although I have seen some ostriches). There is no water out here, so only the hardiest make this their home.

That includes people. The Maasai are different from all the other tribes in Kenya, not only in their dress and their appearance but also in their aloof mannerism. While they are very friendly, they are, nevertheless, Maasai. There is a separation there that can be felt rather than explained, and it has to do with the depth of their secluded traditional customs.

Nevertheless, a light is beginning to shine in the darkness here, and Maasai are coming to the Lord. The darkness that they are coming out of is so deep that it is difficult to fully understand how incredible this transformation is. For untold generations, witchcraft and idolatry have layered curses upon curses on them, and this has caused the separation of the Maasai people from all other tribes in Africa. Throughout Kenya, they are looked down upon and despised as being something less than human, almost a sub-species.

The darkness that has pushed them down is so deep that it makes voodoo look lightweight. There are things in their initiation rites that I cannot write about, they are so bad, and it is just as bad in many other areas of their lives. Their bondage to demonic spirits is as pervasive in their lives as breathing.

This area is so remote that when we finally come upon a church out here, I am stunned. Where do the people come from? It is no wonder that no one has ever come out here to preach the Gospel. It is so much easier to stage a crusade in one of the towns or cities. All you have to do is set up some speakers, have some good music, set up a stage, and preach. Out here, however, you have to work at it to preach the Gospel.

It can be discouraging to drive for hours through miles of rough, dry terrain, choking on red dust to come to a mud-walled church, many times with no roof or floor, only to preach to a dozen or so people. But I'm telling you, the power of the Holy Ghost comes down every time, validating every ounce of effort you have put forth. You leave full and satisfied, knowing that God is here in a power and a majesty that only those who have paid the price to be here can understand. That's when you know that this is the place where you are supposed to be.

I have no idea what God has planned, but I do know He is getting ready to do something here that will confound the wise. And He always uses the foolish things of the world to do it -- foolish things like small gatherings of a despised people way out in a remote place, far from the wiser ways of man.

7 – *Services by Kerosene Lantern*

It's morning out here in the bush. The air is clear and sweet with a faint scent of spice. The sun is strong, and the chill of the evening is fading away.

I've spent the night in a small tent out in the bush because it is too far to go back to town, and we have many more churches to visit out here. Conditions are primitive, to say the least, because the water is so scarce. Water is packed in from wells miles away on the backs of donkeys laden with 5 gal. jugs. The morning shower will be limited to a pan of warm water and a cup to pour it over you. This ain't Kansas, Toto.

But God is here. I wish you could have been here to have seen the Spirit of God descend on services last night. The church service was at 9 pm, long after the darkness had settled over the area, and the only light was from a kerosene lantern hanging from a rafter, but people came filtering in from miles around through the darkness anyway. The light they were seeking wasn't from the lantern but from the Word of God.

How they find their way here is beyond me, but <u>why</u> they do, I understand. Their souls are as parched as this arid landscape. They are thirsty for the Spirit of God and famished for His Word. It reminds me of how they came from all over Israel to hear the Son of God. The prophet Isaiah said that Jesus was a root out of dry ground, and although the Israelites were surrounded with religion, synagogues, and Pharisees, they were still hungry.

The prophets have written that it would be the same in the last days – a famine for hearing the Word of God, and a spiritual desert just before Jesus Christ comes back. (Amos 8:11) There are churches all over Kenya, but there is no revival. Many of these people do not know the difference between church and revival, but they do feel the need for something more than church. They are hungry for God.

And so, they come through the darkness to the light of a solitary kerosene lantern to drink from the well of Living Waters and eat from the Bread of Life.

Today will be more of the same. I will visit two or three churches where hungry souls will have walked for miles and will wait there until I come. The fear that always lingers in the back of my mind is that I will not be able to deliver the anointing that they have come for, that I will not have a message to feed them with, and that the Spirit of God will not flow through me.

But the Lord hovers behind me and whispers in my ear, "When are you going to learn to trust Me?" These are His people, not mine, and it is not me who is going to deliver the anointing, it is God.

And that is why they come.

8 - A Great Light

Evenings here have a soft feeling to them. The silhouettes of acacia trees with their distinctive flat tops stand out against the muted hues of light blues and grays, oranges, and yellows. When the sun sets at the Equator, the darkness falls quickly, and a kerosene lamp lights the room and calls us in for dinner.

Rev. Sampao has been sharing his vision for the Maasai people with me. He himself was a Maasai warrior and has actually fought a lion. One day out in the bush, he heard an audible voice from Heaven commanding him to repent, accept Jesus Christ as his personal Savior, and go and preach the Gospel to the Maasai. That was 30 years ago, and he has been working tirelessly ever since to answer that call.

It has been tough. This tribe is only just now beginning to come to the Gospel because their tribal ties are so strong. When you are Maasai, you are, by definition, separated from the rest of the world. You are Maasai. Their lifestyle is primitive, and their customs are very dark and strange, but their hunger for the Gospel is rising.

Little churches are scattered throughout the bush, the area of sparsely populated backcountry, and they are growing, but many of these Christians do not yet understand much of the Gospel that they believe in. It is a strange situation, but it is simply because they are growing so fast. Their pastors are young and as yet unseasoned, so they are still learning.

The other problem that hampers their spiritual growth is the lack of Bibles, especially in the Maasai language. Even if you have money, which most of them do not, it is very difficult to find the Bibles to purchase. It is the one thing that they need the most and is the hardest for them to get.

The Lord gave me a major word of prophecy during one service that He would lift the curse that is upon the Maasai tribe as they begin to seek Him through His Word. This word came down just moments before I was about to get up and preach. It came down so hard that the brother sitting next to me felt it. This is huge for these people who have sat in darkness for so long. Finally, after thousands of years, God is about to lift this despised tribe of people from the bondage of utter darkness to the liberty of the Light of Jesus Christ. This is a monumental word from God.

Naturally, Satan is doing everything he can to stop this from happening, but somehow these people have an innate understanding of how important this word is for them. They know it is right on target, and that this needs to be their central focus. It's as if they are waking up from a long, long sleep and the morning sun is still a bit bright for their eyes.

But they are waking up fast. And they are hungry. Revival is coming to the Maasai - I can see it in their eyes as I deliver this message to church after church way out in the bush.

Haven't I read something like this before?

"The people which sat in darkness saw great light: and to them which sat in the region and shadow of death light is sprung up." (Matt. 4:15, 16)

He could have been just as well been talking about the Maasai.

9 - Services in the Bush

Services out here are not like anything we're used to back in America.

First of all, the church is rarely much more than a building made with sticks and mud. Some rough-hewn boards hold up a rusty corrugated tin roof that has been cobbled together to keep out the rain. The floors are usually packed dirt, and in some cases, with some crumbled concrete up at the pulpit area. Even in the city of Namanga, few churches are constructed better than that, and quite a few are worse.

But no one looks at the condition of the building. They come to worship God and will walk miles to get here. The cooks get to church early because every service is followed by a meal of rice, beans, and stew, but the rest of the church will filter in during the next 2 or 3 hours. We are on African time, and you have to get used to it. Services will start with only a half dozen people but will end up with 20 or 30. It all works out the same.

There is no electricity, water, or facilities out in the bush, so song service is *a cappella*, sometimes accompanied by a drum and a bell made out of an old automobile ring gear. Nothing else is needed because the rich hues of tone and color of these mingled voices sound like a blended choir many times larger than they are. I'm not sure what creates the fullness of sound, but there is an instant transformation that takes place when they begin to sing. It's as if God honors them as their hearts reach out to Him and mingles their voices with those of angels. You have to be here to experience it.

In every service, the Lord has given me a unique and specific message. Many times, I will speak about things that I had no idea were directed so specifically to the people I would be talking to. They wonder how I knew. I didn't, but God did. And that tells me how important this mission is to Him. He has taken a direct hand in these services and retains control.

A couple of days back in Namanga will give me a break, a soft bed, and some hot showers, and then we will be off to Tanzania for more of the same.

This is not as much fun as it used to be. Camping out in the wilderness was a lot easier 20 years ago. I am beginning to feel my age.

But I can hardly wait to head back into the bush and dive back into the action. The Spirit of God is moving here like an undercurrent in water that shows only a few ripples on the surface and barely reveals the strong tidal forces running beneath it. I can't explain exactly how I know -- I can just feel it. When I wonder about the small turnout for each service, the Lord reminds me of Acts chapter 10 when, in a small meeting just like these, God opened the door to the dispensation of the Gentiles – no small meeting indeed.

In the ages to come, it will be written what has happened here. I am struggling with dirt and poverty, ignorance and desperate need, but I am riding a wave of the Spirit of God as it pours out to meet hungry souls with open hearts.

This is always where God shines the most.

10 - Arusha

We've just arrived in Arusha, the first city on the way to Tanzania. As we came over each ridge, the road would stretch out before us like a straight line through the desert. The wide expanses and rolling vistas to either side feel graceful as they spread out before us.

It is dry – more so than in Kenya – and there are few trees to break up the flow of the land. Every once in a while, you can see a Maasai off in the distance in their brightly colored robes. They are such a contrast against the muted browns, grays, and tawny yellows of the landscape that they stand out even far off in the distance. It makes for a great painting.

Arusha, by contrast, is a dirty city with a mixed pollution of noise, dirt, trash, and exhaust. Few people can be seen with a smile on their face, which puts an additional shade of depression in the air. Maybe it's just a bad first impression, but I am ready to get back on the road. We have stopped here just long enough to purchase some Bibles and will be heading south into the heart of the country.

They told me that the roads are rough in Tanzania. They just didn't tell me <u>how</u> rough. After several hours of a bone-jarring, dust-choked drive down what is supposed to be the main highway, we have found ourselves lost in the interior of Tanzania, somewhere out in a desert. We took a wrong turn, and now we are in the midst of scrub brush, dry grass, and an occasional hyena.

We don't know where we are, and images of running out of gas and getting stuck out here are flashing through my mind. They tell me that there are lions out here. If there are, this could end up being one definitely interesting evening.

But thank God, we got back safely, and although it is late at night, there is a small crowd still waiting for us at the church where I will be staying. They have been praying for us for hours, and a shout of excitement goes up as we pull into the yard.

Wow. Kind of gets you choked up to see how much these people care, and how grateful they are for my coming to minister to them. Just wait until they see the Bibles that I have brought them!

I will be here for a week or two, going from one church to another. I don't know what direction that the Lord is leading, but I'm sure He has a plan ready to go. I can rest tonight knowing that He got us here, and He will use us for His glory.

That's enough to sleep on.

11- African Nights

African nights fall suddenly like a curtain of black velvet. No sooner does the sun set than the shades of night start settling in. The moon rises quickly in a burnt red-orange and soon changes to its usual luminescent yellow.

We are walking back after services through the village in the dark, along a dirt path that winds past silent thatched roofs, sleeping dogs, and silhouettes of mud huts.

When I had arrived at the church earlier this evening, there was a crowd of people in the courtyard outside the church, singing and dancing to the beat of an African drum. There is no electricity or light out here, so this evening's service is held in the glow of a single portable lantern and the light of the moon. What a cool setting this makes!

The choir is great -- singing and dancing in harmony as good as any well-rehearsed group I've ever seen. I am surprised at their level of sophistication way out here in the bush. They may not enjoy the modern conveniences that we take for granted, but these are not ignorant and backward people separated from the rest of the world.

When it was time for me to stand up in the middle of this group, the message poured out of me like a pitcher of oil and opened like a flower in bloom. I don't know how long I was there, pouring out my soul under the moonlight to a crowd standing around me in that courtyard, but it was mesmerizing. What an experience! It was as if God Himself stood in the midst of us, making His presence felt.

As I was leaving, the Lord put a heavy burden upon me for one of the young girls that I saw in the choir. I don't know how to describe how it is that I know when He has something special for someone, but I just know. And this girl urgently needs something from God.

But as I look around, it is so dark that I cannot make out any faces. How am I supposed to pray over someone I can't find in the dark? Silly me. God can see just as well in the dark as He can in the light, and as I turn, I see a faint silhouette standing at the edge of the crowd, and somehow I know that this is the girl. I can feel the presence of the Spirit grow as I approach her, anoint her with oil, and allow the Holy Ghost to pray through me. All sorts of stuff poured out in prayer … and then it was done.

When stuff like that happens, you can't help but wonder what was going on. But it must be one of those "need to know" things, and I didn't need to know – I just needed to do what I was told. A couple of days later the pastor related to me how incredible and right on target it all was, but as I walked away to head home, all I understood was that one of God's little girls needed something from her heavenly Father, and He gave it to her.

The glow is still on me as I walk along that dark path to my bed. I don't know if I'm more lit up over how the Spirit flowed through me, or the prospect of how God is dealing so powerfully with these people. I'm excited to be part of whatever God is doing, and it's obvious that He is doing something.

If this is a taste of what the next couple of weeks will bring, then this is going to be quite a ride!

12 – The Barbaig

I have an interesting tale to tell.

The Barbaig is a tribe in Tanzania that is rather different than other tribes, living on the outskirts of civilization and retaining many of their old tribal customs – like eating elephant meat. Their customs and living conditions are still very primitive and harsh.

Two women from their village walked 11 hours to come to where I was holding services and stayed for 2 days, sleeping in the bush, to attend every meeting they could. I was told about them, but only as a curiosity.

The next morning, however, the Lord dealt with me severely to go to their village and bring the Gospel to them and break the powers of darkness that held sway over their tribe. Someone was praying – and praying hard! And it must have been someone who had some serious clout with God because I could feel the strength of His command. It was not a polite request. It was an order.

Two mornings later, we headed out into the desert to visit their church. Sure enough, there was a small crowd patiently waiting for us. Those women had walked 11 hours back to the village and then continued walking to all their neighbor's homes to bring them to services. Talk about being hungry to hear the Word of God!

This church, made of sticks and mud with a thatched roof, sits at the farthest reach of the Gospel in this area. Beyond this point, no one has heard about the Gospel or anything about Salvation. Islam and idolatry surround them, but nothing about Jesus. This is the edge of the real frontier for Christianity.

Their pastor takes care of three churches that are separated by about 20 to 30 miles, and he has to walk to minister to each one. Imagine your pastor walking all day to get to church in time to hold services, spending the next day walking to everyone's homes to minister to them individually, then walking all the next day to the next church. Remember to pray for this guy the next time you see your pastor roll up to church in his Lincoln.

I asked why no one was willing to help him. Islam holds sway out here, and pastors are targets. Conditions are rough, the work is overwhelming and unending, the hardships and drought have decimated the congregation, and rewards are scant. To be a Christian out here, you have to have a dedication that is real.

In the face of all this, these people have gathered to hear about Jesus from the white man from America. What a service! As usual, God pours out His Spirit in this out-of-the-way place with only a handful of believers in attendance. It's as if this service is special, just for them. As the highlight of the whole service, the husband of the woman who prayed us in here got saved. He had been a lifelong Muslim and had never believed in Jesus, so this was pretty special.

As a reward of thanks, this woman gave me a live rooster. Now, I have never held a live chicken in my hands, so I'm a little put off and ready to offer any excuse not to take it, but the brothers with me here urgently whisper to me that, by all means, DO NOT refuse the chicken. This is a really big deal for this woman.

Um, okay. But how do you hold this thing? And is it going to poop all over me?

To top that, I am taken inside her hut and given a reward of raw honey. I mean raw – wax, goobers, and black things all gooped together in a paste that looks like axle grease mixed with dirt. First, of course, she has to wipe away all the ants and bugs that are crawling all over the jar. Oh, goody! And then she plops a lump of this in my palm for me to lick up.

Dear God, do I really have to eat this?

But she is smiling so hard that it looks like her teeth are going to pop out. How do you refuse something like this? Remember, this is the woman who has some serious influence with God in prayer. So, what do you do? You lick it all up and smile. Oh boy. Isn't this delicious! (gag, gag).

"Oh really? Do you want some more?" As she dumps an even bigger glob in my palm, and I can see Pastor Sampao over on the side laughing his head off.

As I drive off into the dust and scrub brush, they are all waving and shouting to us, thrilled that we had come to visit them. I will never see them again in this life, and I can't help but wonder what will happen here from this point on. I can't imagine some supernatural move of God emanating from this remote village, but maybe that doesn't always have to be the case. Maybe this was just a special gift from God to a faithful woman who knew how to pray.

And maybe that is enough.

13 – Fleas in the Night

It's morning and I woke up to the sound of roosters crowing. I have been moved to another area of Tanzania, and unlike other areas of this country, this place is lush and green.

Below me lies a small valley, patched with different fields. Banana trees, sugar cane, and other crops lie in thick blocks butted up against each other in a long green carpet flowing toward the rising sun, which sits as a huge red ball hanging just above the horizon. Around me are the sounds of roosters from farms all over this little valley and the moans of cattle being roused and moved out of their pens. Birds are everywhere, singing and flitting from tree to tree.

There's also a different scent in the air. Every country seems to have its own distinct smell, and Tanzania is no different. It's not sweet like Kenya, but earthier, like a raw spice. It hangs as a faint hint in the cool morning air, dressing the panorama before me as the valley begins to waken.

The home where I will be staying belongs to a prosperous farmer who is a born-again Christian and has welcomed us in. You can tell that he's wealthy because the floors are made of concrete, not dirt, a major upgrade in my accommodations. Still no power or water, but we make do with batteries and buckets.

The fleas, however, are another thing entirely. As I was lying in bed that night, I could feel all these tickly things up and down my legs. A flashlight under my covers revealed nothing, but as soon as I lay back down, the tickling resumed. I was so tired that I just didn't care and was fast asleep immediately. I wasn't sure if I was imagining this or not, but the little bite marks on my legs the next morning proved that I wasn't going nuts.

While sanitary conditions here may be non-existent, I can pray my way through most of it. Saying grace over meals out here takes on another level of sincerity. A bed full of fleas, however, is beyond what I am able to handle. It is starting to look like the plagues of Egypt – dust, lice, water. What's next? Frogs?

But I guess this is the test. Do I really believe in the desperate importance of the message I am preaching, or is it just an exercise in religious beliefs? At what point do I quit? When do I say that it's no longer worth the struggle? When do I go run off to my nice comfortable home and leave the battle for somebody else? Or worse, just abandon the vision. How much is too much?

It is said that Christianity in Africa was written with the blood of the English and American missionaries who came and gave their lives through sickness, disease, and hardships to bring the Gospel to these people.

I reckon I can handle some dust and fleas.

14 – A Hard Gospel

Three days of seminars and services have had an explosive effect on this little valley we are in. I have cut hard with my messages, but instead of getting offended or mad, these people seem to get hungrier.

Evangelism is unknown to them, but I have put it right before their faces as the primary purpose of their faith. It's as if it had never occurred to them like that, but when I lay out the Scriptures before them, they embrace it with excitement. They really want to do something for God and going out to win souls makes perfect sense to them.

So, they crowd into the next seminar that is going to be about the Word. Instead of my usual message about the importance, the power, and the desperate need for the Word of God in our lives, I have instead turned the message around on them and accused them of laziness. I bring out the example in John 5 about the man who lay by the Pool of Bethesda for 38 years and made excuses of why he never got in the water and point to the analogy in the Bible between water and the Word of God.

I explain to them that the reason they fear the satanic curses of the witch doctors that are all over this area is because they are like Saul's army that went from 300,000 men of war to 600 farmers with nothing but farm tools for weapons. What happened to their swords? Why don't they have Bibles? Like Saul and Jonathan, why do only the pastors have Bibles?

No excuses here. No blaming somebody else. Just hard, in-your-face rebuke, and straight common sense and truth – not sweet-talking, God-is-love mollycoddling. In America, the congregation would get up and walk out offended. Here, they lean forward and cry, "Amen!" They get it. They know it is true, and they want more.

The third service is packed with people from all over the valley to come hear the white man preach. You can't preach it hard enough for these people. No matter how strong the message is, they are hungry for more. You have to love this place!

But it is the fourth service that cracks the heavens wide open. It is 10 pm, and we are in a church with no roof, so we are here under the stars in the dim glow of a lantern. They have come to pray. They want revival so bad that they can't contain the excitement, and you can feel it running through the aisles like electricity.

If you say, "Hallelujah", they shout, "Amen!" If you raise your hands to heaven, they shout, "Glory!" If you say, "Let's pray", they're up on their feet ready to storm the Throne of God. God is coming down tonight to visit His people, and I am standing right smack in the middle of it!

Hours later, we have finally settled down. Chains have been broken, tears have flowed, hearts have been ripped wide open, people have been healed, and God's people have risen to the cry for revival.

Across Tanzania, Kenya, and Nigeria, there are communities and villages just like this, desperately waiting for someone to strike a match and light their fire. I am going to places where white men never go, and where evangelists never consider. It is here that the tinder is so dry and the need is so great that all it takes is a match and the holy boldness to strike it and a fire will be kindled that will burn around the world. Everyone talks about revival, and everyone feels the need, but it takes fire to start fire, and that fire will start here in Africa.

Not every match will stay lit, but I'm striking them as fast as I can, and lighting as many small fires as time and money allow. Soon, it will begin, and a blaze will start to burn in the dry tinder of this part of the world, and it will burn so hot that it will jump oceans and cultures, languages and races. God will pour out His last great revival upon the Earth just before Jesus makes His final return.

When it begins, I will remember the dirt, the fleas, and the hard conditions that I went through, and I will declare that, thank God, it was all worth it. And I'd do it all over again just to see the glory of the Lord revealed.

15 - Explosion

I am deep in an area of Tanzania where no tourists ever come. I am the first white man that some of these adults here have ever seen other than in pictures. The Adults are afraid to step forward, and the kids just stare.

It's not just that whites have never been here before; no evangelists of <u>any</u> color have ever come. It's as if these people are so off the beaten track that they have been forgotten simply because it is too inconvenient to preach here.

I agree. It is inconvenient. For one thing, there are no hotels – at least not what you and I would call a hotel. There is no electricity or running water, no place to eat, no place to stay. Yeah, I'd say it's inconvenient.

But because these areas have been neglected, the effect of a visitor, especially a white man from America, is all that much more powerful. They come to see the white man, but once they come, they get exposed to a stronger level of the Gospel than they have ever known.

So, they come to the first service in the morning out of curiosity, expecting the same old "blessing" message, but they come to the next service that afternoon because they have heard something new and startling. They bring their neighbors to the third service the next morning because this kind of truth is something that their hearts are longing for, and by the fourth service that night, a crowd has turned out to touch the Throne of God. They are pumped and they are energized.

Patience is not my strong suit. I would rather just run through one or two services, deliver the message, and keep moving, but I am constrained to go through with the whole program because I am not in charge – I'm just the guy that does the preaching. Thank God that wiser hearts are dictating the program, because it is that fourth service that always breaks through into an explosion of the Holy Spirit.

Every place we leave has been changed. They will never be the same again. A new vision transforms them, and a newly found faith gives them the lift to rise up with wings of eagles. They believe they can do it; they believe revival can come to them. They know what they have to do to get it, and they are ready to pay that price, whereas a few days ago they never dreamed that revival could ever come to them.

The biggest obstacle these people have had is themselves – they believe God will move in America, in England, in Korea, but not here. Once you break that barrier of unbelief and instill the confidence from the Word of God into them that, yes, not only <u>can</u> God move here, but He has placed His focus upon them, and this is the place where He is <u>going</u> to move. Once they catch that vision, they light up like a Christmas tree. The window of faith opens and all of a sudden, they see a brand-new world. It is exhilarating to see the transformation.

I know I can't reach that many places at this pace – I'm just one guy – but if I can just light a few fires, even if I only touch a few people at each service and ignite them to go forth and spread the vision, then revival can come to Africa.

I believe it will. The people of Africa are such dry tinder for the fires of revival that, if this is not the place that revival will come, then I don't know where it would be. God has to honor their hunger and fill their hearts. He has to. If He doesn't, He is not God.

I believe it's working. It may be slow at first, but it is working. The reason I say that is because, not only can I see the tangible evidence of the working of the Holy Ghost in some very strong ways, but I can see the incredible changes in people's hearts. Those hearts show a reflection of the soul of an end-time revival that is coming to transform these people.

I believe that once a certain flashpoint is reached, the fire will explode everywhere.

And once it explodes, the world will never be the same.

16 - *Miracles and the Message*

There have been times when the Spirit of God would flow so heavily in services that all I had to do was touch someone and they would fall to the floor. Other times, as soon as I would lay hands on a person, I could see into the depths of their heart and know exactly what to pray for. This mission has not been one of those times.

There is a struggle – maybe that's not the right words -- a push and pull, between delivering the Word of God and doing miracles. When miracles begin to flow, people forget everything else and rush to the altar to get their own personal touch from God. All else is pushed aside.

Sometimes I wonder if that is why we see so few miracles these days. Like the crowds that were healed by Jesus, we become so mesmerized with miracles that we forget the reason Jesus came. The Lord actually dealt with me on a trip to Nigeria that there would be no miracles because, if there were, they would not hear the message.

The same goes for Bibles. There is such a desperate need for Bibles that we have to give them to the pastor so he can carefully hand them out after we leave, otherwise, they get in the way of everything else. God sent me to deliver a message to these people, not do miracles and hand out Bibles.

Still, there is a reassuring feeling when you feel that surge of power flow through your hands and someone gets touched by the hand of God. However, when you try really hard and nothing happens, it can be disconcerting.

There was a girl at one of the services who had a bad case of Elephantiasis. Have you ever seen this disease? It's as if some ugly creature with the wrinkled and rough skin of an elephant has latched itself to your foot and won't let go. You just want to reach down and rip the filthy thing off!

I felt like it would be such a simple thing to pray over her and deliver her, but nothing happened. I sure prayed hard enough, but there was no answer from God and no healing. Stuff like that sure wears hard on your heart.

Sure, it's easy to spout off some cute Christian quip about faith, the will of God, or some other canned response but this is not an issue about theory; it is the reality of dire need. When you pray over someone who is sick and is desperate to get healed, but nothing happens, it stretches the strings of your heart and the limits of your faith.

I will never forget praying my guts out over a baby that had Malaria, trying as hard as I could to reach the Throne of God, and then hearing that she died that very afternoon on the way to the hospital. You never forget things like that.

It seems when I try too hard, the miracles stop flowing. Not that they're just running off my fingertips when I am not trying, but it just seems that God has his own agenda, and it doesn't seem to coincide with mine. Anyway, this trip was focused on the message, not the miracles. Only one of the services had anything supernatural take place, and that was the one service that I was not able to bring a message. But what a prayer line we had! Go figure.

Each mission trip that I take has a completely different message and theme, and you just never know what is going to come pouring out of you. But that's when you know that God is actively working through you to reach the hearts and souls of His Church. The transformation of the Church that is needed can only come through the Word of God delivered under the power of the anointing.

I guess that's the real miracle – standing up before a crowd of people and allowing the Holy Ghost to flow through you and pour out of your mouth with a word which you would never have thought of saying. And then, watch it hit home like an arrow in the bullseye of their hearts.

Better to lift these people to a place in God where they can get their own miracles than hand them out like a bowl of soup in a welfare kitchen where they get touched or healed and then walk away back into their life of mediocrity and complacent Christianity.

God is a merciful God – much more merciful than we are – and He knows exactly what He is doing. The trick for me is to learn to trust Him, not only for the message, but for the miracles that He will bring forth in His own time.

John the Baptist did no miracles, and he was the greatest prophet born of woman. That tells you something, doesn't it?

17 - A Great Light

I am heading back to Arusha today, a major city on the way home. We will have one last service there, but my mission is pretty much over. I always get this feeling like a sigh of relief in my soul and from that point on, all I can see is that jet plane taking me home.

The last few days, we have been in Galappo, a small town off the beaten track in the interior of Tanzania. Something broke here. It's never something you can see on the outside; it's something you feel in the Spirit. You can always feel the Spirit of God moving in these services, but only once in a while can you feel that snap when hearts truly break at the foot of the Cross and something supernatural happens to their hearts.

This always seems to happen in places I least expect – little churches in out-of-the-way places. But that's how God has always done it, hasn't He? From a barn in Bethlehem to a Roman soldier in Acts 10, from a fugitive murderer before Pharaoh to a slave in Potiphar's prison, from some fishermen mending their nets to a theological Pharisee blinded on his knees on the road to Damascus – God always uses the small, weak, and despised of the world to confound the wise and mighty and turn the world upside down.

I don't know what will happen here next. I only know that a great layer of ice has been shattered, and souls have been set free to believe. I've done my job and the Holy Spirit has done its work. The rest is in their hands to take this to a greater level in God.

Someday in Eternity, I believe I will meet countless souls who got saved because of what happened here during this past week. I will hear of great exploits that were done by heroes that rose up out of this breakthrough, of men and women who took this message of Salvation to the ends of the Earth. Who knows what God has wrought here? Only Eternity will tell. But I know that a light has shined in a dark place here, and that light will never go out.

As for me, my face is turned toward home. I am looking forward to being there to celebrate my daughter's 16th birthday. As for when and if I will return to Africa, only God knows. It was always in His hands anyway, and it will remain there.

About the Author

Dalen Garris has been in ministry since 1970 during the Jesus Movement in California. In 1997, he began a radio broadcast that ultimately spread to dozens of countries, from Israel and Saudi Arabia to Africa and the Philippines. His program, *Fire in the Hole*, was selected for broadcast four times a week for several years across North America on the Sky Angel network as the Voice of Jerusalem.

A newspaper column followed, for which he has written over 700 articles, which have been published in local newspapers and Christian magazines in several countries. He has also written over a dozen books and several booklets.

Since 2004, he has been lighting the fires of revival in churches spread across sub-Saharan Africa. During the course of 17 years, he has preached in over 1,000 churches and has seen hundreds of them set on fire and explode with growth, and hundreds of new ones planted across Africa.

Hundreds of people have been supernaturally healed during the healing lines that so often sprang up during these revival meetings, and tens of thousands have been saved. And the fires are still burning.

Because of his work across Africa, Dalen Garris was awarded an honorary Doctorate in 2017 by the Northwestern Christian University of Florida.

Dr. Garris currently lives with Cindy, his wife of 43 years, in Waxahachie and is still heavily involved with churches across Africa.

His pressing hope is in seeing this powerful move of God in Africa ignite us here in America to see those same revival services that made such an explosion in Africa. He believes that this upcoming generation will be the Gideon Generation that will usher in this last, great revival that he has preached about for so many years.

Brother Dale, as he is known across Africa, has settled in Waxahachie, Texas, with his wife and three grown daughters and their children. You can contact him and find his pamphlets, books, videos, and podcasts at www.RevivalFire.org.

If you would like him to speak at your church or organization, please contact us for times and schedules. We do not charge, nor will we ever charge, to preach the Gospel anywhere in the world.

He is willing to take this message anywhere people are hungry for a God-given, Holy Ghost revival.

Books by Dalen Garris
(revivalfire.org/books)

- Four Steps to Revival
- Do You Have Eternal Security?
- Standing in the Gap
- Two Covenants
- Fire in the Hole

Revival Campaigns

- The Kenya Diaries
- A Trumpet in Nigeria
- A Scent of Rain
- Into the Heart of Darkness
- Fire and Rain
- Revival Campaigns in Africa – 2019
- The Battle for Nigeria
- A Match in Dry Grass
- A Light in the Bush

A Voice in the Wilderness series:

- vol. 1, the Journey Begins
- vol. 2, the Early Years
- vol. 3, Prophet Rising
- vol. 4, Revival in the Wings
- vol. 5, Sound of an Abundance of Rain
- vol. 6, Watchman, What of the Night?
- vol. 7, Mud and Heroes
- vol. 8, Ashes in the Morning
- vol. 9, Shaking the Olive Tree

RevivalFire Ministries

PO Box 822
Waxahachie, TX 75168
dale@revivalfire.org

http://Revivalfire.org

www.ingramcontent.com/pod-product-compliance
Lightning Source LLC
Chambersburg PA
CBHW070451050426
42451CB00015B/3444